ENTED Decade

W9-DCF-847

HURON COUNTY LIBRARY

For my father, James

THE DEMENTED DECADE

THE MULRONEY YEARS - WHAT REALLY HAPPENED...

RAESIDE

Doubleday Canada

Canadian Cataloguing in Publication Data
Raeside, Adrian, 1957 -
    The demented decade : the Mulroney years

ISBN 0-385-25453-9

1. Canada - Politics and government - 1984 -
Caricatures and cartoons. 2. World politics - 1985 -
Caricatures and cartoons.   3. Canadian wit and humour
Pictorial.   I.Title

NC1449.A33A4   1993   971.064'7'0207   C93-095053-4

Printed and bound in Canada by Best Gagné

Published in Canada by
Doubleday Canada Limited
105 Bond Street
Toronto, Ontario
M5B 1Y3

1

Joe Clark
The 272-day Fiasco and Trudeaumania
Part Deux — the Return of the Living Dead

Joe Clark was a classic example of the you-cartoonists-are-so-cruel-to-him type of politician. Clark was never destined to make the cover of *GQ*. He did, however, come really close to having his own chapter in the *Book of Failures*. Observing the Clark government was almost like watching a traffic accident in slow motion: you see what's going to happen; you can't stop it; you don't want to watch it, but you do anyway.

While the Tories were being toe-tagged and carted away, Pierre Trudeau triumphantly returned to 24 Sussex and filled the swimming pool. After pillaging the country for a couple more years, Pierre called called it quits and gave the unpleasant task of burying the Liberal Party corpse to the Liberal's version of Joe Clark — John Turner.

Elsewhere in the universe, Ronald Reagan continued to scare the bejesus out of us by keeping a firm grasp on the nuclear button and a tenuous one on reality.

Q: BUILT INTO THE SOPHISTICATED EARLY WARNING RADAR SYSTEM, SENSITIVE SURVEILLANCE SATELLITES AND COMPUTER CONTROLLED CHECKS,...IS A WEAKNESS THAT COULD CAUSE THE ACCIDENTAL LAUNCH OF THESE MISSILES...
WHAT IS IT?

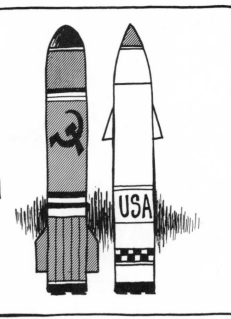

Victoria Times Colonist. RAESIDE © '82

A: ...A COUPLE OF LOOSE NUTS.

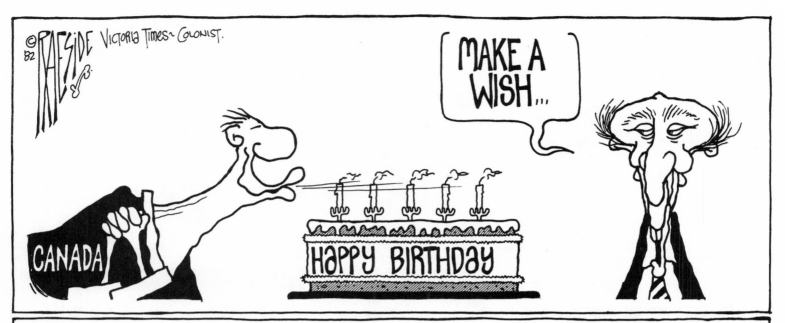

2

Enter Mulroney:
Same Old Trough, New Snouts

In 1984, Brian Mulroney finally realized his life-long dream and succeeded in stabbing his way to the top of the Tory heap. He annihilated Turner and the Liberals at the polls, largely by spewing righteous tirades against previous Liberal abuses of patronage. But Brian's decorators had barely finished installing the fun-fur toilet seats at 24 Sussex, before a second sitting was scheduled at the patronage trough. What had started as a genteel nibbling at the taxpayers' pockets quickly became an orgy of piranha-like savagery.

Meanwhile, Ronald Reagan continued his campaign to eradicate any Central Americans who didn't vote Republican.

©'81 RAESIDE Times-Colonist.
CANADA
YOU ARE HERE
NATIVE INDIANS

ROBBERY THROUGH THE AGES... THE STONE AGE:

RAESIDE Victoria Times-Colonist

THE SEVENTEENTH CENTURY:

THE NINETEENTH CENTURY:

THE TWENTIETH CENTURY:

CABLE COMPANIES

CABLE BILL

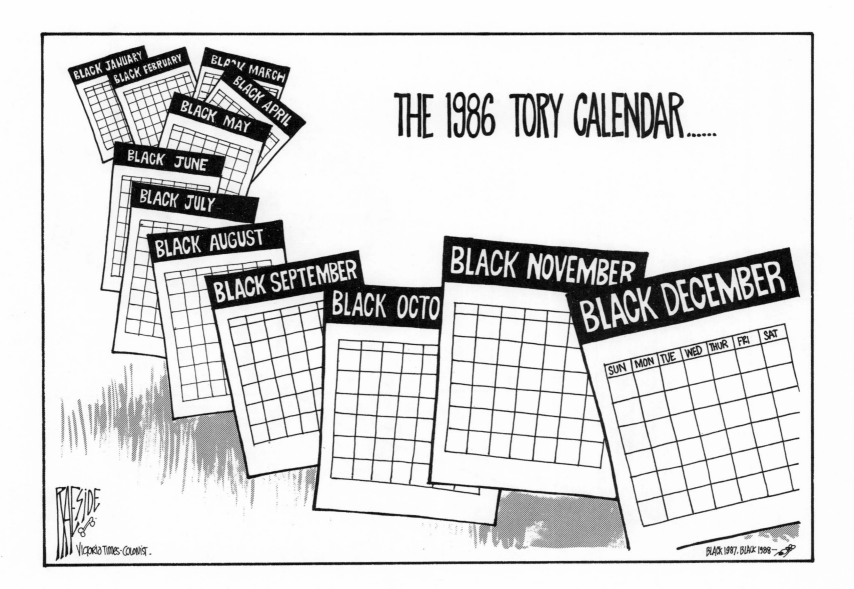

3

Free Trade:
The 3,831,033-Million-Square-Mile Garage Sale

Like typhoid, the idea for a free trade agreement between Canada and the United States seems to appear every seventy years or so. By the late eighties, the plague was beginning to surface again. Eloping with the U.S. became an obsession for Brian Mulroney. Who can erase the memory of an unctuous Brian, draped over Ronald Reagan, croaking out "When Irish Eyes Are Smiling" ? Saddest part is, Reagan thought he was in Cleveland and didn't have a clue who Mulroney was.

As alarm grew over the budding romance between Brian and Ronnie, Mulroney was forced to call an election over the Free Trade Agreement. Turner and the Liberals (the NDP might as well have taken the month off), seeing a chance to redeem themselves, did their best to ward off the forces of evil, but in the end, Mulroney got a renewed mandate, Turner got the boot and the U.S. got the rest.

In other news, the stockmarkets went into the sewer and more bodies were found in El Salvador's dusty streets — full of U.S.-manufactured lead.

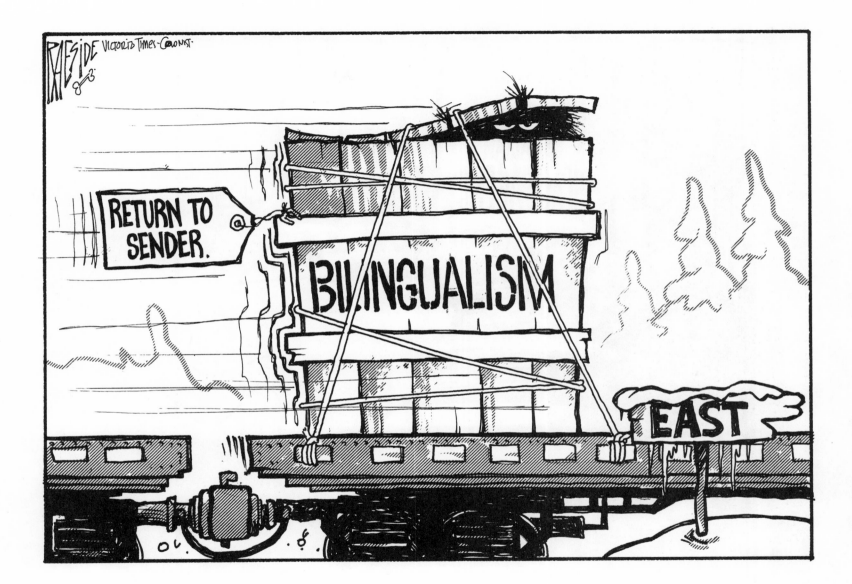

BANK STATEMENT OF SERVICE CHARGES.....
Victoria Times-Colonist.
RAESIDE
We have all your savings. If you want to see them again give us $23.00 per month. Do not call Consumer Affairs
The Bank
WE'LL LET THE TWENTIES HAVE IT FIRST.

IN THE NEW 'HUMANE' SEAL HUNT, SEALERS WILL BE USING RIFLES INSTEAD OF CLUBS....

Warnings we'd like to see on cigarette packages....

RAESIDE Victoria Times-Colonist.

WARNING:
IF SMOKING DOESN'T KILL YOU, THE NON-SMOKER SEATED NEXT TO YOU PROBABLY WILL.

WARNING:
SMOKING CHANGES THE BREATH- REDUCING YOUR CIRCLE OF FRIENDS.

WARNING:
IF YOU CONTINUE TO POISON YOUR SYSTEM WITH THIS PRODUCT YOU MAY END UP OCCUPYING A SCARCE HOSPITAL BED. CREATING A BURDEN ON AN ALREADY OVERCROWDED HEALTH CARE SYSTEM.

EXTRA MILD

SMOKES

MILD

OF FOREST COMPANIES ARE HANDED THE RESPONSIBILITY OF MANAGING B.C. WILDLIFE.....

Victoria Times-Colonist.

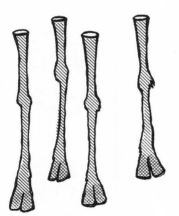

4

The GST:
(Or How To Succeed in Alienating Twenty-Six Million People, Kill Off Small Business and Destroy the Economy of a Previously Prosperous Country Without Really Trying)

With the federal government bulging with highly-paid Mulroney cronies, the national debt defying belief and Mila Mulroney's kamikaze shopping trips becoming more frequent, a new, more lucrative source of revenue had to be found. Despite the economic disaster that universal sales taxes had inflicted on other countries that had tried them, the Tories went ahead and introduced the Goods and Services Tax anyway, employing the same sensitivity and finesse they had previously used in driving through the Free Trade Agreement.

Introduction of the GST had one positive effect, however: it woke the Liberal-dominated senate from its hundred-year slumber in order to block passage of the bill. Only by stacking the senate with his chauffeur, hairdresser and family dog, was Mulroney finally able to pass the bill.

In the Middle East, one fly-blown dictatorship invaded another fly-blown dictatorship. This would not normally be cause for alarm, except that in this case, both countries were sitting on enormous oil reserves. Canada, because of its commitment to the U.N., and extreme beneficence, became part of an international force sent to protect the multinational oil companies' bottom line.

LET'S SNEAK THROUGH THE WOODS TO CHECK WHAT THE ARMY'S UP TO.
USING ANCIENT MOHAWK STALKING SKILLS
LIKE GHOSTS WE CAN GLIDE THROUGH THE FOREST UNDETECTED...
WE BECOME PART OF THE LANDSCAPE.
RAESIDE Victoria Times-Colonist.
TV
NEWS
TV
NEWS

Mike Harcourt's Range of Emotions....

Victoria Times-Colonist. RAESIDE

 THOUGHTFUL

 ANGRY

 HAPPY

 OUTRAGED

 OVERJOYED

 DEVASTATED

 REFLECTIVE

 FURIOUS

 AMUSED

 IRATE

 STEAMED

 TICKED OFF

 EUPHORIC

 ON THE WAR PATH

 MAD·AS·HELL

 SERENE

 FRENZIED

THE STEERING GROUP ON PROSPERITY REVIEWS SOME SUGGESTIONS ON HELPING CANADIANS GET RICHER....

Get rid of Mulroney
evict John Crow
TURF OUT MULRONEY
abolish the Senate
Scrap Mulroney.
Do Away with THE GST
VAPOR'

GIVE MULRONEY THE BOOT
Fire the M.P.'s
Trash Mulroney
FIRE JOHN CROW.
DUMP MULRONEY
Retire WILSON
Retire Mulroney
'nt the senate
'D MULRONEY
Tories

Deport Mulroney
Scrap Free Trade
SEND MULRONEY TO MARS
Abolish the GST.
TRADE MULRONEY
Scrap the Tories
Fire Mulroney
Abolish Revenue Canada
SELL MULRONEY
Do Away with GST

ACROSS NORTH AMERICA, CITIZENS ARE PROTECTING THEIR PROPERTY....

7 P.M. EST JANUARY 16, 1991

VICTORIA TIMES COLONIST

* CLEARED BY MILITARY CENSORS.

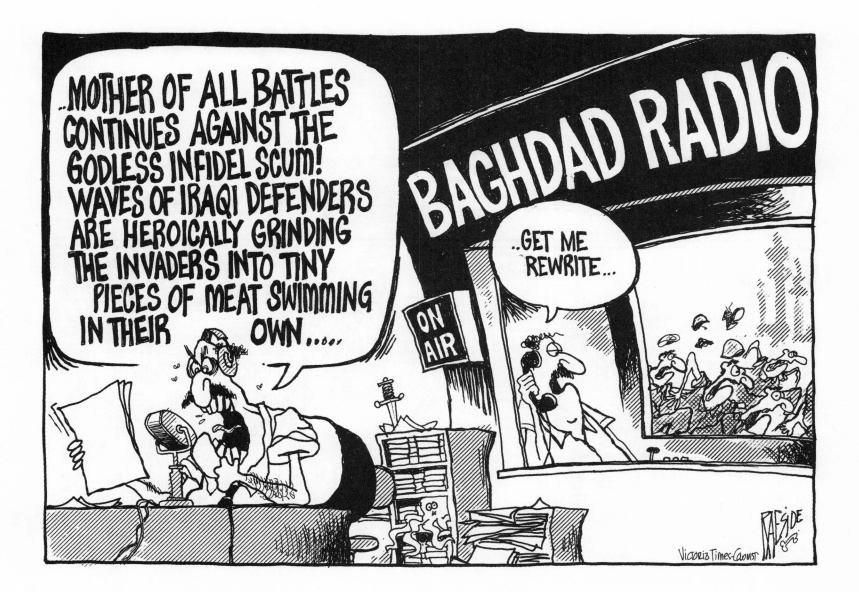

As I said, I have to be careful not to plagiarize myself.
Although tin cups and Russia seem to go together so well. . . .

FTA:

NAFTA:

5

Rolling the Dice:
Making a Clean Getaway

Mulroney, anxious to get Quebec's "Jean Henri" on Trudeau's constitution, subjected Canada to month after month of endless, pointless (and expensive) travelling committees and constitutional conferences. All this did was employ armies of normally unemployable constitutional experts and lawyers. The madness finally ended with a national referendum on the Charlottetown Accord. Canadians were to vote on a compromise originally put together by a small group of provincial premiers held hostage for a weekend on the shores of Meech Lake.

Despite threats from the Tories of disembowelling and deportation for those who said "no", Canadians voted overwhelmingly to trash the accord. Mulroney boasted that he had taken a chance and had "rolled the dice". (He wasn't exactly betting the farm – he'd already sold it to the U.S. a couple of years earlier.) It was only a matter of time before Brian and his gang of four hundred slipped out the back door of 24 Sussex, leaving Kim Campbell with some tatty furniture and the unpaid rent.

Western aid programs....

Band aid:

ETHIOPIA

Live aid:

FLOUR

SUDAN

Blockade:

IRAQ

Victoria Times-Colonist.

RAESIDE

The P.M. checks Tory standing in the polls...

DEALING WITH SADDAM HUSSEIN'S U.N. VIOLATIONS...

THE EVOLUTION OF THE NDP IN CANADA....

CANADA POST DELIVERING A FIRST CLASS LETTER....

CANADA POST DELIVERING A PARCEL...

CANADA POST DELIVERING OVERSEAS MAIL...

HI MA.. HOW'S IT GOING?..

CANADA POST DELIVERING LOCAL MAIL...

CANADA POST DELIVERING JUNK MAIL...

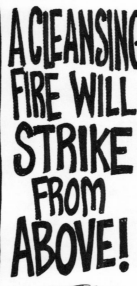

With the results of the referendum coming so close to press time, I did three cartoons in advance, covering the possible outcomes: yes, no and maybe.

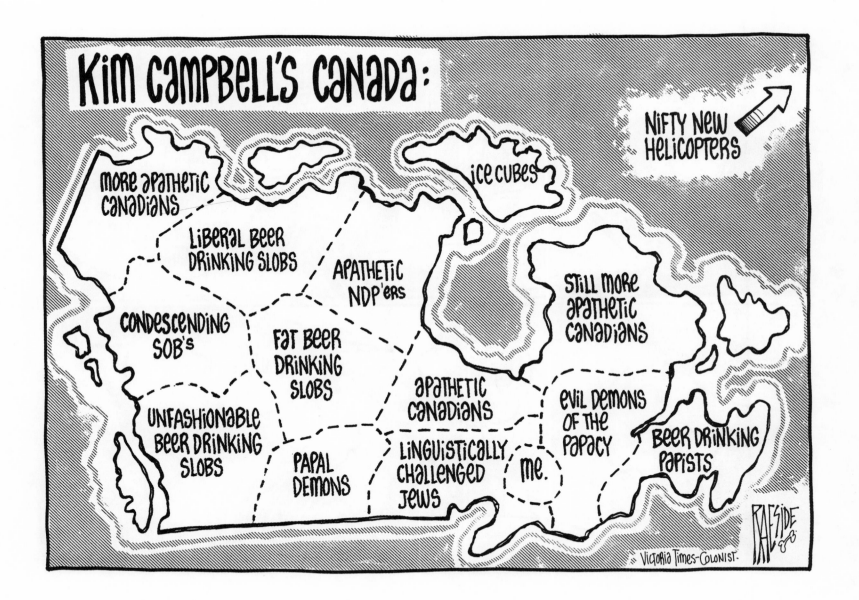

Also by Adrian Raeside